SOMEONE SPECIAL

Edited by

Sarah Andrew

First published in Great Britain in 2002 by
POETRY NOW
Remus House,
Coltsfoot Drive,
Peterborough, PE2 9JX
Telephone (01733) 898101
Fax (01733) 313524

HB ISBN 0 75434 349 9
SB ISBN 0 75434 350 2

FOREWORD

Although we are a nation of poets we are accused of not reading poetry, or buying poetry books. After many years of listening to the incessant gripes of poetry publishers, I can only assume that the books they publish, in general, are books that most people do not want to read.

Poetry should not be obscure, introverted, and as cryptic as a crossword puzzle: it is the poet's duty to reach out and embrace the world.

The world owes the poet nothing and we should not be expected to dig and delve into a rambling discourse searching for some inner meaning.

The reason we write poetry (and almost all of us do) is because we want to communicate: an ideal; an idea; or a specific feeling. Poetry is as essential in communication, as a letter; a radio; a telephone, and the main criterion for selecting the poems in this anthology is very simple: they communicate.

CONTENTS

WHITE FLOWERS

White flowers
I bring
Recalling hours
We spent together
In laughter,
In tears.
White, pure
Like the gift
You gave of
Yourself, flower
Of your personhood
Unfolds now
Beautified in memory.
Seasons turn,
Warmth and calmness
Touch me here
Where you rest in
The heart of holiness
Reaching me
Quietly and in peace.

George Coombs

FOR MY FATHER

A silence has fallen between us now
With only the echoes of memory.
At a concert the applause must end
And those who were enraptured together
Will walk away alone.
'He would have liked this' is often in my mind
And these were the chords we struck together.

You were not my advisor in chief,
For you kept only the beat of fantasy,
Revelling in the wild doings of the world,
Delighting in mischief, though you made none.
But the bell that you rang was true and pleasant and tuneful
And more to be missed,
Than many a deeper or a louder chime.

Annette Turner

LOVE

Friendship is a thing that lasts,
love has been around and is meant to last.
Once it happens, it's like a spell,
it can make you feel unwell.
The pain in your heart is like a dull ache,
especially when you make the break.
If love was really so sincere,
you would never have to fear.
It makes you feel in another world,
with hope, light and beauty around.
It's so final, the finish of love,
the world that is left is like being above.

E M Backham

SING TO ME ON-LY WI-TH THINE EY-ES

He was told by his teacher at school
never, ever, to sing with the choir
as he put them all out of tune;
what was the use of a vibrant voice
when it jarred on the nerves of others?

So, cursed also with very short sight
'specky four-eyes' all his friends chanted
teacher putting him front of the class
facing the group, back to the blackboard
reciting from memory till all were bored.

Playtime and football, glasses on teacher's desk,
quite good at dribbling, ball at his feet
foxing his opponents - and foxing himself!
Pleased with the cheering - but mistaking the caution
passing the ball to an opponent who lobs it into goal!

Genetically gifted a superb brain
yet interpreting clear directions
through a dubious range of senses
giving rise to misunderstanding and coarse laughter
until that day he met a face over the playground wall.

That afternoon he lingered going from school
happening to meet her leaving piano lessons,
facing her again, confounding turning to proof
how, he so miserable when she had gone
now proving their two hearts beat as one!

And I will pledge with mine!

J Lucas

MY ONLY LOVE

My only love is lost to me
Gone forever more
No more his sweet face will I see.

What did I do that made him flee?
That made him walk out the door?
My only love is lost to me.

My tears have fallen steadily
My emotions are all at war
No more his sweet face will I see.

I tried to picture him desperately
I tried, but no one I saw
My only love is lost to me.

I asked him back, but fruitlessly
It hurt me to the core
No more his sweet face will I see.

There is no other apart from he
Of this I am sadly sure
My only love is lost to me
No more his sweet face will I see.

Clare King

YOUNG LOVE
(For John my husband-to-be)

Beaming faces.
Soft embraces.
The world you surrender.
Your manner soft and tender.
Worries and cares seem trivial,
And drift as it were into space.
Our deep romance, seems to fill their place.

Everyday life to us, seems artificial and droll.
Passionate flames of fire burn within my soul.
I cherish your protection more than any earthly thing.
Our love is far more than documents,
And a gold wedding ring.

When you are absent for a second,
My world begins to turn,
Without you I am helpless,
And I yearn for your return.
The thought of you so near,
Makes me courageous, brave and strong.
I adore the very ground which you tread upon.

Our moonlight kisses,
Indicate how much you care.
Your gentle, caressing fingers,
Running through my silky hair.
Your arms clasped tight around me,
Instinctively protecting me from harm.
The starry sky above us
So tranquil and calm.

Your love for me is unique,
And cannot be described.
It has such a depth and meaning,
And without it I could not survive.
Our love will be eternal, flourishing on
Forever and ever.
For nothing can sever the ties that bind,
Our mutual feelings for one another.

Emma Jane Thackway

SAL

I always see her smiling face,
In gardens where roses grow.
Warm as the sunlight was her embrace.

When I see the rivers race,
She is visioned in the flow.
I always see her smiling face.

I walk along at gentle pace,
Beside corn in summer sun show.
Warm as the sunlight was her embrace.

She lies behind a veiled lace,
Hiding her from me although,
I always see her smiling face.

For me she is a constant grace,
In a loving afterglow.
Warm as the sunlight was her embrace.

Gone now to this other place,
No more days can Earth bestow.
I always see her smiling face,
Warm as the sunlight was her embrace.

Elwyn Johnson

QUEEN ELIZABETH, THE QUEEN MOTHER

August 4th 1900, a future queen was born,
They called her Elizabeth Bowes Lyons,
Her family used to own Bowes Museum,
Such a wonderful museum.

She married Prince George,
Future King of England.
Then she became queen,
How popular she was with the English!

When her husband died,
She must have wept and cried,
But life still goes on
And she was strong.

For a whole century she lived,
And she had kids;
Her eldest she named after herself,
She was to become Queen Elizabeth.

She has always been popular and well liked,
Of all the royal family she was the most liked.
When she died aged nearly 102,
It was the biggest tragedy of 2002.

Margaret A Greenhalgh

I WILL LOVE MY DAD FOREVER

As I walk down the alley
I can feel a shiver down my spine
I turn around to see if anyone is there
But no one is in sight

I hurry along, listening to my feet
Making a shrill sound
Like the rustling
Of the brown and scarlet leaves

I keep on walking
I am almost there
I wish I could go faster
But my legs cannot bear

A few steps more and I am home at last
I open the brown door
And sitting there is my dad
With worry in his eyes

I run to him with everything I have
With every bit of strength
I leap in his arms
Put my arms around him and feel his protection

I know I am safe now
I know no one can get me
I wish this moment would never end
I wish this moment would last forever

He kisses me on my cheek
His moustache makes me tickle
I feel warm and cosy in his arms
I will love my dad forever!

Sonya Nikolosina (14)

ALWAYS MY LOVE

Shall I compare thee to all that's good
For taking care of me, making me feel loved?
Marriage is about loving and giving
We had all this and much, much more
In time of difficulty your love overpoured,
All through my recovery
My sickness, my moods
You never even blinked an eye,
My mastectomy was radical
My scar is now my life.
I'm really proud that you're my husband,
So glad that I'm your wife.

Caroline Halliday

MUM, WE NEED YOU!

Mum's on strike!
Very soon
Crumbs gathered in the kitchen
Carpeting the floor,
Mixed with a few spilt drinks.
A porridge-like mess
Soon appeared
Which stuck to everyone's feet
And almost
Glued you to the spot!
Mum,
Where are you?

The dirty dishes began to smell;
Rubbish began to pile up;
We didn't feel like eating!
In fact
There was no 'proper food' -
Just junk food
Straight from the cupboard.
Oh, for a decent meal!
The stuff we always
Complained about before!
Mum, we miss you.

The bedrooms were in disarray;
Toys strewn everywhere,
Mixed up with sweet wrappers,
Felt tip pens with their lids off,
And dirty clothes.
How it got so messy
We will never know!
Mum, we really *need* you.

The bathroom was 'the pits'.
Grime inside the sink and bath;
Dirty, damp towels,
Unwashed clothes,
And worst of all,
The toilet!
It took a brave person
To enter there!
Mum, you *must* come back.

Cobwebs everywhere
Spiders in unexpected places,
A trail of ants
Discovered the crumbs;
Mice, too,
Found their haven.

Mum did come back,
When things were at their worst.
Only when she was gone
Did we appreciate her,
And notice how much she did.
No one
Could take her place.

To all the mums out there
Who sometimes may feel
Like giving up:
We need you!
May you know,
Deep down,
What a great job
You do.
God bless you.

Sue Trickey

LOVE YOU FOREVER

The four seconds we spent together was
never less for me.
Sometimes you weren't there
sometimes I wasn't there.

These long summer days have never been
so dizzy to me before.
After a long time our moment has come,
we both can recall our past well.

A feeling has touched the corners of my heart,
I wish to say something to you
but my voice gives in.

I was never always this selfish before.
How could I forget you?
Even if I die, your name would be
the last thing I say after the Lord's.

You know I haven't betrayed you.
I will always be with you in an untouchable way.

Parveen K Saini

A MESSAGE TO FAY (FROM GRANDMA)

You were ten days old when I held you for the very first time,
with ten tiny fingers and ten tiny toes.
Auburn hair and a turned-up nose.
As you grow with your sisters you will have such fun
with a devoted daddy and an adoring mum.
When you stumble on the way along life's rocky road,
your fall will be cushioned with an abundance of love.
I will watch with pride when you learn to walk
and listen in wonder when you start to talk.
You are my third little grand-daughter, but darling you are unique,
you will make your mark with the world at your feet,
and whether we are close together or far apart,
you will always have a special place in my heart.
With love

Brenda Rollo

A TRIBUTE TO THE MEMORY OF HRH PRINCESS MARGARET 1930-2002

She was too young at 71,
To die,
A young princess of royal grace,
Why - was *she* the one?
We all get old.

Three score years plus ten,
The Good Book says,
To look back and then
Remember all those, of elder years,
And when we've gone,
Just fight the tears,
And remember.

J Harper-Smith

LOVE

Love is in the air?
    Not for me it isn't.
It's due to leave me far behind
    For now the sky's the limit.

God help its flight,
    To hold on tight
Too many limitations
    And then to wend its way back home
with love and felicitations.

Beth Spinks

FEELING LOVED

Feeling loved is when your bare arms are wrapped around me
So loving and tender.
We snuggle up in sweet silence
Just savouring each moment, each thought
With no words passed.

Feeling loved is when you care for me,
Support me and comfort me in my times of need
You are always there for me,
Waiting, to reassure my soul.

Feeling loved is when you affectionately kiss my forehead
Whispering sweet nothings in my ear.
And when I look deep into your crystal-blue eyes,
I can see deep into your heart
Where there is a safe haven for me.

Feeling loved is when your rose-red lips
Gently meet mine,
And we are connected for a single second,
Two of us become one.

I will always feel loved by you.

Jessica Murch

CHILD'S LOVE
(Dedicated to Rashida Khatoon & Mohammad Hassan)

Lovely life - fellow human being
I think of you, Mama, all the time
You gave me love, care and life
Devoted your time, sleep and wishes.

I think of you, Mama, all the time
Changed my nappies, washed my bottom
Gave me a bath
And fed me the precious milk.

I think of you, Mama, all the time
I suckled your milk two and a half years
But you did not stop me
I think of you, Mama, all the time.

You have your life to bring me up
You spent your endless time to feed me
To cuddle me and teach me
I think of you, Mama, all the time.

You gave your whole life to make my life
I think of you, Mama, all the time
You loved me so much as no one loved me
I think of you, Mama, all the time.

of every person's every moment's
kaleidoscopic life's livings.

Afifa Khatoon Eqbal

GRANT ME LOVE

My love for you is so imperfect.
It feels as though the heat of the day,
Shall cause it to wither away.
The only way I know to make it grow,
Is to love you all the more.
If I say a word unkind,
Through reckless and selfish thinking,
Water me with loving patience,
Until I am refreshed.
If I argue with sinful pride,
Nourish me with simple kindness,
So there's no room left
In my heart for madness.
If I fail to be tender or understanding,
Hold my hand
So that I may feel your warmth.
Above all, share with me
The sunlight of your smile.
For in all these things,
A man's spirit cannot help but grow,
And in all eventuality,
All tears of the heart
Shall be wiped away.
Showing in time and season.
A more perfect love.

Ronald D Lush

SPARKLY EYES
(For green eyes)

Sparkly eyes
Gentle sighs
Touches of fingertips
Kisses from passionate lips
Caresses down my spine
Feelings sublime
Moans and sighs and noises
Distinctive murmurs. Distinctive voices.
Instruction. Suggestion.
Full body devastation.
Joining, merging.
Discovering.
Images drifting.
Senses shifting.
Until. Gentle sighs.
Sparkly eyes.

Teresa Whaley

UNTITLED

The world stood still,
All folk were blue,
They'd lost their Queen Mum,
Queen Grandma too.

The children were sad,
With posies and tears,
The elders looked on,
Remembered past years.

But then from the Heavens,
The sun shone - as never before,
And everyone realised
Their Queen Mum and Grandma
Would reign evermore.

She was perfectly happy,
And astounded to see,
Her wonderful people all bonded,
In harmony.

A life's work well done,
Britain at its best,
She smiled and waved goodbye calmly,
For now she could rest.

June Bradbury

ONE IN A MILLION

I look at you my old friend and wonder what you feel
Do you remember the hard times, the pain and anguish we had?
I like to think I saved your life, and somehow, you were mine
Named for the child who later left me
What is in a name so special?

Nurtured, and loved for your very eccentricities, then kept
Later, distraught, mother killed, but on realising you were left,
Just relief it was not you who was taken
Sixteen years, just living, being there, sometimes a pain,
Mostly a funny, loving, trusting little friend

Growing older, more a pain, but younger days still showing through
Remembered times of frolicking,
Silly moments of re-lived joy and fun
Other people now entranced with your very own personality,
shaped by myself and our life together

Daniel, you've been more than one in a million to me
Born a feline, but more a character than most human beings
This charisma seen by those close to me
I've loved you so very dearly, not shown to you enough
I hope you know how much I care

Times when you left home for days,
Did you capture someone else's heart?
Or were you just locked in a lonely shed?
Causing tears and fears and worries and sleepless nights
On rare occasions when you were ill, countless rockings in my arms

Please stay with me my little friend, amidst the tears
Your lifetime has been long and well treasured
Stay with me a while longer
We still have life to live and love together
My well-loved little friend

Joy Walsh

LOVE IS . . .

First touch, first kiss, initial bliss
Unwrap a brand new toy
Exploration, excitation
Discover love is joy.

Familiar face, a warm embrace
Together all night through
Safe, secure, honest, pure
Discover love is true.

Uncertain days, more time, more space
Intensity, intrusion
Crazy, mixed up, what to do?
Discover love's confusion.

Indiscretion, wrong impression
Jealousy, desire
Taunting, flirting, hating, hurting
Discover love is fire.

Time apart, a beating heart
The card that never came
Ringing phone, no one home
Discover love is pain.

Friends' advice, all very nice
Won't ease a troubled mind.
Tears are shed, whatever's said
Discover love is blind.

Despair and fear, so far, so near
So right and yet so wrong
Redeem, reclaim, relight the flame
Discover love is strong.

The ups and downs, the smiles and frowns
The driving up the wall
Sweet nothing or curse, for better or worse
Discover love is all.

Andreas Koumi

To A Little Red-Haired Fisher Boy I Once Knew

You were born as my best friend's little brother,
I remember the day.
Your dad was a ice cream man then.
I was nine.

He gave us treats because he was happy to be your daddy.
You were a tiny red-haired sweet terror,
Not at all like your blonde sisters.

You ran around causing trouble
At our school parents' evening.

That's all I remember until you were 12.
I saw you fishing by the river,
'Growing up nicely,'
I thought.

You said 'Hello' and remembered me,
And left my last memory of you
By the riverside.

Roxie Willows

FAR AWAY

Can you smell the fragrance of the rose
I picked, but never gave you?
Did you hear me whisper
I love you?

The kiss I blew
Did it touch your lips?
I know I am not so far away
When I think of you.

When you are asleep I hold your hand
Till light of morning breaks.
Outside, can you hear the blackbird
I asked to sing my serenade to you?
And do you notice
How all the flowers smile at you?

When the evening mists have gone
Look up at the sky and behold -
All the stars that twinkle
I asked to wink at you.

The wind that blows and swirls around you
Is my embrace
And the rainbow my everlasting promise:
I will come home to you.

Brian

B E Leaman

A HAND TO HOLD

We shared a flat together,
But we never shared each other.
We were just friends,
Friends of the very best kind.
We were often mistaken for brother and sister,
It made me feel beautiful,
For beautiful he was.
He made me a brass hand-shaped pendant
As a token of our friendship,
Before we went our separate ways,
Before we moved out and moved on.
I still hold fond memories of him,
And when I feel insecure
Or let down by life,
I find him in my dreams.
His smile made me smile.
And now I think I know
Why he made me that hand -
It is for me to hold.

Caryn Saunders-Squires

GOODNIGHT QUEEN MOTHER

Saturday, 30th March 2002, what a tragic day it was
The whole country was in sadness
People turned out in their thousands
To see the Queen Mum for the last time
They showed tears of sadness that the Queen Mother
Had passed away
A smile of happiness for the wonderful life she lived.

The Queen Mother was a lady who had courage
And was loyal to her country and people
She lived a fulfilled life right up to the end
The magnificent 101-year-old lady whom we all loved
Both the royal family and the Bowes-Lyons will miss her terribly

You could hear the tremble of the drums
And the skirl of the bagpipes
As the Queen Mother's coffin made its way
To Westminster Abbey
The sun shone brightly upon the country and people

She has now gone to Heaven
Where she will be with her beloved Bertie
The Queen Mum has lived her life to the full

Goodnight Queen Mother.

Jamie Kee (16)

ALONE

Torrid rage, stormy sea
Have they all
Forgotten
Me?

Abandoned, discarded
Can't you
See?

Is there not
Any love
In your hearts
Left for
Me?

Open your door
Cherish me once
More

Light my heart
Lift me up
In your arms
To be
Kissed

Solitary figure
Standing by
The shore
Is there any hope
Left for
Me?

A cry of a gull
Pierces this heart
I thought that we
Would never
Part.

J Ashford

THE DAY I MET THE QUEEN MOTHER

She came over to me and I was
Standing in the crowd with my flag
I was waving my flag,
She gave me a smile and wave, when she went on her way,
I will always have a memory of the Queen Mother.

Roger Brooks & Jane Docwra

A Mother's Kiss

A mother's gentle kiss,
Softened with a sigh.
Smooth and sweet against a cheek,
Her fragrance from the day.
Sends a child off to sleep,
In a mother's special way . . .

Russell Bassett Stanley

FOR PAST LOVES

Like a cat to fireside
My mind returns to you alone
To curl up where the airs collide
And mix warmly and rise in tone.
The edges of the day subside
Like beats rejected from a poem,
And you are all I see and feel.

As clothes fall from a body, fall
The dropping aspects of the last
Material defensive wall,
And settle on the floor dispersed,
The edges of my selfhood pall
And drop away to leave the first,
The single form that they conceal.

And so by flight of memory
I drop the weight that age puts by,
Remember what it was to be
Essential as the blood, as high
And drunken as the bumblebee,
As naked as the open eye,
Like an orange, from its peel.

I know I lost you as you are,
Your body, your immediate kiss,
And I don't know you any more
Which makes a mockery of this,
But I remember what you were
And I remember utter bliss,
And it was good and it was real.

Tom Crowther

SOME PEOPLE'S ROMANCES

Leaf
I can smell the great outdoors
upon you
I smell your seasons
and your fear
of
falling in autumn

Leaf
I smell your father's bark
I hear the song of
soaring skylarks
in your
spidery veins

Leaf
I hear the nightmare wind
that is swift and keen to cut you
as you cling
to your ancestor's branches and

Leaf
I feel your mother's earth
the soil and the true dirty glorious dirt
silently shifting but making
the best of your chances

Leaf
I see the sun on your back
And your shining shellac
and the love and the looks
and the glances
of some people still
young in their romances.

Graham Adcock

WHEN WILL WE MEET AGAIN

How much longer do you intend to hide yourself?
Your email shocked me
How many more sleepless nights
do you want me to suffer?

What's the big deal
to change from one subject to another
to talk with a counsellor
to meet friends and family

Will you recover
after letting yourself down so long?
Where's your sweet smile?
When will I hear your big laugh again?

Are you really wanting to give up *everything*
even your family, friends and future?
Being nineteen is just too young to put a stop

Don't you understand
Can't you wake up
Cheer up, my darling
And set your goal again!

Mei Yuk Wong

THE QUEEN MOTHER

All of 101, who on this Earth, a long course has run?
Our Queen Mother has done very well,
She has stood the test of time, and so graciously too, might I add,
                                                    truth to tell
And for 100 years, a whole generation! Indeed such a spell,
Many, thank God, were made aware of, just how well and able, she was
Our queen supported too, many a good cause
She was a good queen? Indeed that she was!
She was so very human with it, yet so able
She honoured too, and consistently to, be true
The Christ Child, I hear, born and laid in a stable.
Of the Queen Mother's attire I never did tire,
Those ostrich feather hats, I truly did admire
This lady, born a true lady, lived in the kingdom,
Here too, in bonnie Scotland, she was known by more than a few.
She seemed so frail, so vulnerable of late,
Yet so determined even in her gait, still determined to,
                                    whatever her fate, to much aspire
Yes! In her still, was such a fire, never mind a spark of life
She, though a queen, a mother and a wife,
Was right alongside us, through Hitler's war, bloody gore and strife
Scotland will miss, this once wee Glamis lass, aye
Who brought, no doubt to life for many, some true meaning to life
                                                    forbye.

Margaret Lightbody

FOR GRAHAM

When the leaves fall,
And the sun shines,
They see your face,
Not as it would be now, but as it was
When the first bloom of youth,
Touched it with rounded beauty.

Your heart was golden,
Lit with mischievous fun.
Woken by the rich tapestry of life,
Unaware of darkness or gloom.

Yet light did pale to dimness,
Within so short a span,
When boyish dreams and hopes,
Turned into the despair of man.

Now flowers bring you nearer,
Helping to soothe the ache.
When the leaves fall,
And the sun shines,
They see your face.

Beryl L Lambert

WATCHING

Seated in an upper room
At a window filled with green
I look through the window sash
Through the green
And watch you moving through the garden,
And my watching is as if we had never or not yet met;
Gentle hands raise a weather-beaten rose
And I watch and I watch
Looking down on love.

Julie Wakefield

April 9th, 2002

It was a day I shall remember
A day of sadness and regret
A grand old lady to those who loved her
And those that she had met.
But when I watched her funeral
I had to sit and stare
I realised that I was one of those
   who didn't know I cared.
I felt a sense of sadness
Now that she has gone
And those that lined that sunny street
Seemed several miles long.
I wish I had also been there
And been one of those she'd met
A day I shall remember
Yes a day I'll never forget.

Renalta Hall

To Spend But One Minute In Your Arms

To spend but one minute in your arms,
A minute, so short in appearance,
A mere grain of sand in the beach of life.
Yet with you,
It could simply wash away and it would not matter.

To spend but one minute in your arms,
Time would grind to a halt,
Yet it would still not be enough to appreciate your form.
Your look is of pure divinity as it shines a light
Into the tunnel along which I trudge,
Looking for salvation.

To spend but one minute in your arms,
I would be complete.
The final note would be played,
And my symphony of love for you
Would be heard throughout the land.
The world could be held in our hands and pushed aside,
For my love for you would conquer all.

Steven Stroud

OUR BABY

An adorable little lady
with beautiful blue eyes
gurgle, hiccup, gurgle baby
and sometimes little cries
with hair, o' so grand
and a cute little nose
and so tiny hands
perfect are your tiny toes
our little God-given gift
with smiles so bright
give our hearts a certain lift
but please sleep through tonight!

Seth P Mansfield

A MOMENT OF TIME

An old man shuffled along the path
Keeping just in the light of the sun
His thoughts were still bitter and dark
As his mind wandered back one more time

His love had left him when he was young
His children had grown up and long gone
His heart once full of passion and life
Was now - oh so cold and so sad.

Then perhaps by some chance or by fate
He noticed an old lady approaching - so slow -
As she came nearer they both stopped and turned
Was it possible? Oh yes! It was Her.

Even after all these years they both knew
Tears trickled down his old wrinkled face
The old lady - dry-eyed - she just bowed
Then she looked up - but no words were said

They both had their own private memories
Which they both thought were now all dead
Their eyes met again for one brief moment
But they just looked and then turned their heads.

Transfixed in that *moment of time*
The old man turned and walked on his way
When he reached home he was very distraught
The agonies of time would not go away.

Then he gave out one last cry of pain
And after all these years, at long last
To end this long *moment of time*
He laid down and died from his broken heart.

Margaret Luckett-Curtis

To Mother

She knows
She knows the feelings, innermost, of those assembled here
   The heartbreaks and jungles of curried emotions
   The tugs and gut-wrenching memories of time
   Eroding onto souls like gemstones clenching to
   Mountainsides
She knows

She knows the truths, tunes and workings of us all deeply
   Tempers, tastes, argumentative ways of many
   She's the holder, the family judge presiding
   Ruling carefully, weighing the arguments of the accused
She knows

She knows the past, present, pastimes, of children and men
   And has danced in the merriment of them all
   Drinking red wine with laughs and guffaws
   Jollying in the presence of all members, friends dear.
She knows

She knows the way the heart pounds and jigs to the music of life
   The bellows of lungs, in, out, in, berating those who
   Oppose
   The aches and agues of time over the human living body
   The ways of wrinkles and folds of skin on the female form
She knows

She knows the hugs, happiness and holdings of those so close
   The warmth of kin, kindly, carefully comforted
   By her all-encompassing love, without questions
She knows

She knows that we too take and receive this love without question
   Grasping and cleave to its very deep origins and roots
   Such overwhelming depths of purity beyond the human
   Mind

She knows

She knows we love her beyond all imaginings, worldly, interminable

She knows we know.

She knows.

Martha Watson Brown

A TOAST TO THE LATE QUEEN MOTHER

Queen Elizabeth, the Queen Mother,
Whose life I watched with pride,
How she helped her husband Albert
Through decisions, by his side.

Albert, crowned King George the Sixth,
And Elizabeth, his queen,
How the country is so proud,
For the good things they have been.

Their children, Elizabeth and Margaret,
Two princesses loved by all,
Elizabeth, now our queen,
Has steadfastly played her role.

We really are so privileged,
And envied by so many,
For we have our British heritage,
And our royal dynasty.

Her courage and convictions,
Carried through her life's career,
Her laughter warm, infectious,
Gave joy, and cured despair.

Her loved ones grieve so deeply,
But know the rewards they reap,
From being blessed so greatly,
For great memories they can keep.

The Queen Mother lives forever,
Within the nation's hearts,
She holds us all together,
United, as on her new path she departs.

Monica D Buxton

FILIA TERRAE
(To H from B)

Lift your soft head and let me see your face -
wherein is writ your secret book of life -
where laughter, love and glad acceptance chase
away the tears and yesteryears of strife.

Here Magdalen's sad eyes (whence glimpses stray
of love's lost battles) winsomely do shine;
here lips (where rue and truant kisses play)
with love's hot hunger now impassion mine.

Whilst some will wear life out in search of truth,
and crawl cold-hearted to an empty grave,
you in your lovely, last, resistless youth,
each moment cherish and each new breath crave.

Would that I could my questing mind subdue,
lock up my life, my destiny in you.

Bernard Brown

MY OLD FRIEND

How I miss him, that old friend of mine
He was with me I remember most of the time
Unless he went hunting for a mouse or two
Sometimes out in the fields in the morning dew
Yet if I called, he would always come
Calling to me in the evening sun.

A J Marshall

A Different Reality

You have given to me a brand new world,
Which glowed with brilliant incandescence
And encompassed the sweet promises of life.
To find that life lived in the glow of your essence.

The heat of your body invited me to snuggle nearer,
As you nestled closer, my arms wrapped about you.
I turned to regard your beautiful face,
Only to realise I'm nothing without you.

'Twas you whom drove me to unbelievable passion,
The love I had always dreamed of, so rare.
In return I gave you all I possessed,
With my heart filled with dreams for the two of us to share.

As we shared all our laughter and heavenly delight,
Before the fire of passion swept us into ecstasy,
Paradise here we come, together, my darling, together,
Now whirling me through a different reality.

Whilst my arms were crushing your body to mine
And my mouth was brushing your hair,
I whispered so softly, these urgent words,
'My darling, you've answered my prayer.'

An intensity of pleasure and fulfilment,
The like I'd never even dreamed of before,
I love you my princess, my angel, my own,
Please know it is only you I adore.

Your kiss is as sweet as the nectar of the gods
And I know I'll go on loving you, the rest of my life,
As your lips opened beneath mine, my darling,
I whisper the question, 'Will you be my wife?'

M J Plummer

ENTIRETY
*(In loving dedication
to Val and Errol)*

Through times, as now,
When I sink . . . to depths of aloneness,
And to no avail, try to fight
The enveloping cloud,
I need you so much,
Just to fill the emptiness with the warmth of your arms -
To replace the cold
By reaching for my hand,
And seeing through my silence.
Just simply to know me.

And yet, in so many ways,
You are everything -
Everything I feel,
Everything I know,
Everything I breathe.
My world, in so many spheres,
Consists solely of you,
And I fight the urge to call out your name . . .
To deny the borders . . .
Just to run to you.

And failing,
I reach out and touch you across
Deserts of separation,
Because I realise,

You're all that I am.

Tavyn Chalmers

LOVE

The perfect fit, love
climax of equality
creation's honing.

Robert D Shooter

NEFERTITI

Ethereal you stare into space
As if you can see what we can only dream of
You seem timeless - your beauty astounds
As precious and unique
As the hands that created you so long ago.

Perceptions of Amarna captured in that *look*
Somehow your New Kingdom 'era' fits this New Millennium too
And the sands of time span the gulf between your world and ours.

Graceful Nefertiti are you in some long forgotten paradise still?
Wandering amongst the avenues of time . . . or waving
      serenely from the window of appearances?
Maybe your are cradling your children protectively and smiling at your
husband in the sunlight . . . worshipping together whilst the *rays* of the
sun-god wash over you weaving an aura of magic?

Is that why you look so exceptional even now?
The sculptor created your image so perfectly didn't he?
For that *look* will haunt all that look upon your beautiful face
For all eternity.

Elaine Edgar

JULES

Something pushed us together
It's all very scary!
Every day we find something else
We have in common, uncanny.
When you kiss me, I feel the fireworks
Inside me, my heart dances,
It's like we float off somewhere
Out of this world, with the stars.
You smile at me constantly
Your emerald eyes hypnotise me,
Your red mane smells of fresh poppies
As it brushes my face, soothing.
Strolling on the beach this weekend
Was magical, the waves touching us.
It's funny how nothing else matters
When we are together, breathing each other.
I feel so warm when you hold me
And I know something special has happened,
Like two pebbles drifting along a beach
Toward each other as if it was meant.

Craig Shuttleworth

TO THE MEMORY OF DIANA - PRINCESS OF WALES

A beacon of light in a world grown dark,
A pillar of love, in a careless time,
She was given so little but, gave her all;
To the afflicted, down-trodden, outcast and poor.

She gave with compassion, to the old and the young,
A sympathetic hug for the bereaved;
A healing touch to the sick;
She strived in her own quiet way, for a better,
More peaceful world to grow forth.

No accolade did she crave for that which she did;
She just prayed she could make a difference;
May we, follow the example Diana set;
As we go along our pathway through life,
Let us, add to the essence of her love and light;
So, healing a world of darkness, trouble and strife.
Nothing is lost, much can be gained by following
An excellent example.

Frederica Greenway

HEARTS

A heart is such a tender thing,
So easily bruised,
An unkind word or cutting look,
It feels it all, love is such a healing balm,
A touch, a glance, a squeeze of hand to the poor, lonely soul,
A million dollars could not buy.
Rare indeed, is this sweet and lovely thing,
One heart that to another talks in dear
Sweet harmony.

June Sweeney

WHEN CHILDREN LEAVE HOME - MOTHER'S LOVE

One who loved you as a baby,
One who enjoyed seeing you grow up,
Being proud of you as you grew up,
One who enjoyed you being around,
One who always loves you,
One who wants you to be happy,
One who is always pleased to hear your news,
One who is always pleased to see you,
One who always cares,
One who misses your absence,
One who hurts when you are not there.

Joy Marshall

UTOPIA OF DREAMS

Love was always meant to be
Utopia of dreams
That sings ones heart-adorning thoughts
Romantic gestures from the heavens
To gleam a starlight in ones eyes

Its magnetic sway commanding
Bringing weakness to ones knees
Euphoria so beautiful
Jubilation I believe
That tells the mind, yes life's worth living
For true love is meant to be

Birds that gather for a chorus
In a tranquil sunlight bliss
Echo charms to countless lovers
As they stroll the valleys green
Their paradise in all its glory
Dreams of true love meant to be.

Maurice Ferris

I CAN IMAGINE

I can imagine Thomas eating his
sausage, egg, chips and beans
. . . with his hands.

I can imagine his impish grin
as he wipes those hands
. . . on the curtains.

I can imagine Thomas at the other end of the phone
saying 'Knock-knock Daddy'
and me saying 'Who's there?'
and Thomas saying 'Me!'
. . . as he replaces the receiver.

I can imagine Thomas's clear blue eyes
fill with tears as he cries for me
. . . and the joy on his face when we're together.

I can imagine Thomas
stumbling, frustrated in his disability
. . . but getting there in the end.

I can imagine Thomas . . . my son . . . my future
. . . as we walk hand-in-hand
from the past.

Ted Medler

WEDDING BELLS

Hear that eerie sound - echoing around -
Listen to the message that it's sending.
It's seeking you to bless - with joy and happiness -
To fill those days with love - never-ending.
Even doves that coo - if too, they only knew -
Would sing - like nightingales in springtime.
They would keep in tune - they dare not rest too soon -
Before two hearts are one - forever entwined.
Exchange the golden ring - angels above will sing -
Blue's a patch of sky - everything is bright -
And listen to the beat - the tappings of the feet -
Welcome the deep peals - of sheer delight.
There's music rich for two - the future's bright for you -
For every song that has been sung - brings a word of joy -
Give your love quite free too - promise to be ever true.
And always leave some inner self - a part of you that's coy -
For when the day is over - the bells will stop and rest -
And the life you now will lead - will be heaven-blessed.
Still floating on the breeze - will be notes that tease
And in the final beat will be - a message clear -
Never turn your back upon - the life you have now -
And always say a loving thing - making sure he's heard.
Smile at him when talking - smile at him when sleeping
Smile at him when walking - or when not in his sight -
Smile at him while eating - smile for ever keeping -
A special smile at waking - and see him smile at you!

Valerie Cubitt

LOVE

No doubt, love is the best
rest is meaningless, forget the rest

door of the heart is open
allow him to enter as special guest

I cannot escape his sight
who cares it's east or west.

It is happening it'll happen
feelings exist love will make its nest

it is only reflection of the sky
can waters pass this test.

Noor Shahzadi Alam

UNTITLED

From steel to azure, skywards fell
the day I held your hand
foolish tears, blue raindrops burning
painful pleasure, faintly yearning
sea-horses on sand

dreams come, dripping down the day
seeping snake-like into night
- that curse! Now etched onto each breath
overwhelms (such tenderness . . .)
- take flight! (Too late) - Take flight!

Beating, fearful, always fearful
mists appearing, no more land
tearing hesitation, waiting,
on and on, sea-horses breaking
over your reluctant hand.

Christine Titmus

HOW I LEARNT TO MISS YOU

Sadness the moment I took off
As if I left her forever
The moment I landed there
I cried never, never and never

How naive I to know
Until I left her land
Gone to viva Espana
For sun, sea and sand

I daydream her whole day
At night I make her picture
My mate, my guardian, my soul
My love telepathy please reach her

How can I live without her?
Now the true moment has come
I am truly empty without her
And my body function numb

Many she flesh white, golden and brown
Swimming, peddling, tanning on deck chair
Nothing compare to what I seek
My beautiful for whom I care

The beach looks so romantic
The sound of waves at night
Looking at the stars and the moon
I stare in trans imagining her sight

Lone beach stroll ever so hurtful
I get tired of being alone
Just her my righteous pride
I write my poem to mourn

My days are on the countdown
Impatiently await to reach her land
Forever lasting embrace and kisses
And never to let go her hand.

Phil Ellison

SHADOW PLAY

Does the swaying candle flame make you recall
One boundless winter's night
My love?
And the rain and the tempest,
Does it deprive your form, of security
My love?
Do your pale hands fasten the quilt
About your demure frame
And infuse a prayer for me?
Pursue the dark tracery
Of the iron bedstead;
Conjure those contours
Into white filled islands
Where I place woven baskets
Cascading sweet tropical fare,
Into your arms, bedecked
With adornments worked from exquisite shells.
Your breath, white in the acid air
Is to me like the thudding surf.
I hear your heart beating in every wave descending.
Wish for me the days into weeks, the weeks into months
My love.
I yearn to hear the timbers and haul the sails aloft,
Set the prow for Old England, a crackling hearth
And, my love.

Wendy Milner

WHAT 'WE' IS

Our hearts are one, a harmonious beat
As they share the very same key,
Our minds are equally captured
In togetherness both of us free.
Our emotions are swirling, yet peaceful
Passionate, loving, secure,
Our souls are the infinite partners
On an eternal journey, for sure.

Christine Rooth

LOVERS' MEETING

I sat alone in the church garden
When he walked up to me
Music was in the air, a string quartet
Were playing my favourite Tchaikovsky.

He sat down beside me, as if he knew me
And for me it was exactly the same
I didn't need an introduction
I instinctively knew his name.

How could it be? I'd never met him before
But there was no doubt at all
As he touched my hand I just knew
That we had met before.

He was 30, I was 60
To return it had taken so long
But he knew as soon as he looked at me
That our love was just as strong.

The last time I'd seen him was well in the past
We'd been sailing that day at sea
When a squall blew up and he had been drowned
But someone had rescued me.

We were young and in love, too happy to last
But we'd pledged that as long as we breathed
We'd be as one and when he was gone
All I could do was grieve.

Now he had found me but I am old
How cruel fate can be
I can't give him now what he clearly needs
When he is only 30.

Pamela Baily

THROUGH SICKNESS AND HEALTH
(For Vivien, when she was ill)

Despite bad news, the pain that bruised through no fault of your own,
As we prayed our love grows stronger, preparations are being made.
Will we fade? There's the chance, but it's not the option that once
Threatened to consume us. The truth? It's never an option at all.

We're special and unique, but to the world just a bizarre antique,
Even elders consider us lost in the greyness of a century ago.
What is love to the many? Just the mass of saccharine lust
Paraded before red eyes through media, TV and on film.

Around us now, true love is quaint, written off like historical saints,
Rare, barely seen distinctly unobscene, cherished like
                                    impossible dreams.
Self comes first. The other is good, but to be burnt like
                                    paper if spurious,
Considered a fence with restriction, an obstade in fiction,
                                    now too serious.

Your illness shook me up out of the pettiness of work,
Your sweetness echoed through his canyon, where I lurked,
Where I counted the hours every minute of my time,
Wanting each day to end with some true peace of mind.

When you take my name, this wait will be over,
The test of purity complete and unbroken three years over.
Commitment has stayed, God has pulled us through doubt,
We will not have much, but with each other won't be without.

Andrew Sanders

FORBIDDEN LOVE

Shall I compare thee to a sip of wine
Full-bodied, fresh bouquet . . .
Perhaps a sultry evening breeze
To wash my cares away?
I long to stroke your silken hair,
Caress you through the night,
Whispering sweet nothings
Until the morning light.
It grieves me much to turn you down,
for it surely would fulfil me . . .
but alas should it come to pass
my darling wife would kill me.

W Ballantyne Scott

CUDDLES FOR COMFORT

How I love the sweetness of youth
The gentle hand patting me on the back
The butterfly kisses on my cheek,
The unconditional affection given by one child to another,
The giving, the pleasing, the willingness,
The helpful little soul.
The little trier, doing his best to score a goal.
The master and the little miss all know how important
　　　　　　　　　　they are to Mummy and Daddy,
Even if they have a paddy all they really want are cuddles
　　　　　　　　　　and not puddles of tears.
For all the tears the king of all babies is a proud little boy
And the queen of all babies is a proud little girl.
It is comforting to know we treasure our children.

C V Bennett

FORTY YEARS OF LOVE

She was naughty at first this girl I met
Blue eyes flashing in the bright sun which seemed to say
'Do not talk to me'
But barriers are meant to be broken
She relents at last,
We dance the night away,
Courting now begins.
Love comes knocking on our hearts,
Marriage bells toll the message that
Love has triumphed once again
Forty years on this year of Royal celebration
Our love grows stronger and stronger
And may Mother Nature prolong this
Love for another forty years.

David Bromage

PICASSO

Picasso 20th century
Master
Painter of love, passion,
Horror and disaster
Lean Blue years and
Pink circus laughter
Cubist classic innovator
Invented art like a sunburst
(To quench the vultures' thirst)

Celebrated creator
Maker of sculptures, prints
Ceramics of nature
Cheered and held in reverence by his people
He plundered El Greco, Greek myth and
Africa
Then mixed it with his Spanish blood
Only age forced him to throw down the glove.

Graham Peter Metson

ANDANTE

Love must go on, like a rumour
of new love -
an invented grace.
The heart is veined,
auditioning.
What is broken must be healed.

Through my life
the days stand up,
a year of appetites tasted or bemused,
drinking the wine of summers,
living where the sun rises
in the country of love.

I fear no exile - only time.
All the clocks are ticking:
life is greatly loved.
Ordinary life is holding a man
holding a woman;
speech - and no words.

What is broken must be healed.

Simon Richardson

ROGET

Born London, 1779.
Progeny, male child, offspring, descendent, son,
Inheritor of a Swiss divine,
Ecclesiastic, preacher, clergyman, shepherd,
Minister, leader of the flock and pastor
At the French Protestant church,
Threadneedle Street.

Medical student, Edinburgh U,
Graduating at 19.

Gained reputation, name, renown, celebrity,
Lustre, prestige, distinction, fame and station
Through medical research into nitrous oxide
Used as an anaesthetic.
That's laughing gas to you.

Founder, Manchester Medical School.
Fellow and Secretary, the Royal Society.

A closet lexicographer, he drafted
His Thesaurus in 1805, keeping it
Secret, private, clandestine, restricted,
Confidential, classified, occult, purely
For personal use for almost fifty years,
Publishing it in 1852.

Early editions offered frank and open
Synonyms for sex; sexual congress, sexual conjunction,
Sexual intercourse, love-making, the idiosyncratic
Junction. That's an odd one. Junction?

His vice was altogether otherwise and elsewhere: verbs, adverbs,
Utterances, neologisms, phonemes, ideophones, expressions, nouns,
Coinages, barbarisms, synonyms, conjunctions, nonce words, words.

Endless, retentive, priceless stores of squirreled, hoarded words.

Norman Bissett

Us

Friends introduced us
as natural partners,
belonging together,
fulfilling each other,
matching like gloves.

Our meeting I sensed
as destined as dawn's
succeeding the dark.
I felt the joy of Columbus
on sighting land at last.

We began to know
one another, the unfolding
of buds here around us
in the springtime, then suddenly
the garden aflame with colour.

But a young love starts out
is a fresh wind: overnight
it may change its course.
We drifted apart, not yet
seeing our bounty of luck.

Soon I became
a sailor becalmed, anxious
for the wind's return.
My calls unanswered, I grieved
in a vale that gave no echo.

To exist without love
was barren; desert sands
devoid of all life;
walking empty streets at night,
cut off from all around me.

Then you called to say
you loved me still. All at once,
life returned to life!
Merriment and joy galore!
Loudly sound the trumpets!

Roger Mather

LOVING FEELING

I hate being in love.
It gives me an icky tummy.
My insides turn to putty.
Then I then get nervous
The fever gets worse and I start to shake
And I don't feel so great.
I feel like I'm going to be sick.
I don't think I like this feeling.
I feel more like an alien than a human being
And my skin's turning green.
I feel kinda seasick as love sails the rocky seas.
I feel like I've been stung by a thousand bees
And the doctor said 'Love ain't for me.'

Laura Sansom

THE FAVOURITE

The horse whispered to his brother,
'I just can't run this race,
I miss the dear Queen Mother,
She's not in her usual place.
How can the crowds expect me,
To give my best and win it?
Oh, they'll cheer me on,
But, with her gone,
My heart just isn't in it.'
The jockey sensed his sadness,
And stroked the shining mane,
And said 'Come on, old lad,
She'd be so glad,
To see you win again.
She always did her duty,
And ran a lengthy course,
So, do your best my beauty,
For you are the Queen Mum's horse.'

Patricia Davies

LIFE GOES ON

Dear M
My life began when I met you,
You won my heart,
You showed me life
I wish you were still here.
I miss the fun,
I miss the closeness,
No one can predict their future,
But one day, I will be strong
And rebuild my life,
Forever miss you in my heart,
Like the tide on the shore flows away,
It comes back.

Pauline Willicombe

THE GREATEST LOVE STORY 1997
GUNPOWDER TEA

Your Majesty, Your Royal Highness, i
A humble subject with the name of George
Respecting royal glasnost will now forge
A sonnet that shall praise you to the sky
On your immortal Anniversary.
Greatest love story! i need no more enlarge
But crave your gracious favour to emerge
From sweet obscurity, 'Take counsel and take tea'
'Stir gently, pour and savour,' the advice
From Messrs. Twining Est. in seventeen six
'Appointed to your Majesty' how nice!
But leaves your loyal subject in a fix.
Tea without milk? Confound such knavish tricks!
Gunpowder tea and glasnost will not mix.

Mel Pomene

SEASONS OF LOVE

I remember you in moonlight
When stars lit up the sky
Night of sweet enchantment
Forever firefly.

In sunbathed hills of flowers
I picked a rose for you
Its perfume filled my senses
We promised we'd be true.

Then in autumn's colour
The gently falling leaves
Fall with all my tears
For you my heart it grieves.

As when the snow in winter
Lay in drifts of white
You left me for another
My heart it died that night.

Brenda J Hoskin

LOVE ALPHABET

Alluring, attractive, amorous, amused
Benevolent, my baby, I believe in you
Charming, considerate, cool and calm
Delightful, deep, desirable in my arms

Embrace you, encourage, enlighten all expressions
Feelings, fantasise, feel free from all repression
Giving, gaining, a gallery of memories
Harmonious, heartfelt, high, almost heavenly

Intimate, insatiable, in love, imagination
J, just you, jellybeans and jubilation
Kind, keeping kisses keen
Loving, my lover, lush, lively, lean

Magical, meaningful, melodic minds meet
You are my north, nocturnal thoughts, a never-ending beat
Open optimism of a love deep as the ocean
Pleasing, pulsing pleasure in a palm of pure emotion

A quotable quality, quest not to be quashed
Radiant, romantic, reflectiveness awashed
I'll be your south sensual, sensitive, with a smile
Touching, tearful, babe hold me for a while

Understanding, unexpected, uptight until united
My valentine vision, you'll always be invited
Warm, waiting, with whittling wishes
X times a thousand, sending my kisses

Yonder yellow sunset yearning for you
Z, last but not least, I love you.

Hayley M Morris

GRANDAD

It's been 20 years since you have been in my life
And although I know you are watching over us all
I can't help but feel it's unfair that you had to go.

The few years of my life we had together I don't remember
I have been told how much you cared and loved me
But it's unfair that I can't ask you.

I have been given some of your things
And Nan tells stories of you
But it's unfair you're not here to hold me when I need you.

One day I know we will be able to see each other
One day we will be able to hold each other
One day we will be together.

Why did you have to go?
I love you Grandad.

Francesca Elliott

EQUATIONS OF LOVE

It's useless asking questions now, there
can be no replies from the other side of life,
if there is any.

Even here, you had stopped answering
when my late rebelliousness
barred your way. You were taken aback
by the change in me, at my challenging
the partiality of your love for sons over
daughters. How you tackled my persistence!
If any discrimination at all, you said, weighing
it carefully, it couldn't be more than
the difference between 19 and 21, almost
nothing if any at all, you pointed out, such
was your craft, enough to disarm the fiercest
adversary. But not me. I still went on, finding
more ammunition to break down your motherly
reserves. By the time I was hit by the truth
of reversals - 19 and 91 instead, I became sure -
you were gone, safe beyond my childish
tuggings, after all these years of growing up.

And now despite the lightness of your numbers,
the burden of love weighs me down.

Rani Drew

ELIZABETH BOWES-LYON - A LOVE STORY

Born to the family clan of Bowes-Lyon,
An infant of destiny grows into childhood,
Fairest of face and vivacious of temperament.

When war comes she puts aside games and enjoyments,
Her home is transformed to a military hospital,
She tends with compassion the sick and the wounded.

War horrors cease and the guns become silent.
A debutante now, she emerges in loveliness
And attracts the attention of shy young Prince Albert.
Determined to win her, he waits with great patience.

Her marriage with 'Bertie' and two little daughters
Makes everything perfect. As Duchess of York she
Fulfils public duties with charm and devotion,
Delighting her husband, her children, her public.
But one day their 'world' falls, collapsing around them,
For Bertie must face, he is heir to the throne!
With the greatest reluctance they accept the inevitable.

King George the Sixth, with his precious Elizabeth
Move from their home into Buckingham Palace,
They take up their duties and win much affection,
When war is declared they stay on with their people,
Consoling the injured and bombed out Eastenders.

After the peace, and some blessed years together,
Elizabeth suddenly finds herself widowed,
She picks up the pieces, is titled Queen Mother and
'Magical Grandmother, gloriously unstoppable.'
'Incredibly kind' said Prince Charles, 'And I loved her.'
Now farewell sweet lady, the pride of your country,
Serene in God's love, with your 'Bertie' for ever.

Nancie Cator

LOVE CONQUERS ALL

When interviewed on camera
I was rather bemused
his rhetoric was cutting
toying with fools.
An immediate interest
in his kind of style
defensive, melancholic,
lacking a smile,
evasive and solitary,
in a world of his own,
signals were caution,
a no-go zone.
Except at a function
his manner was stony,
friendship and love
an obvious phoney.
Eventually acknowledging
our very existence
chauffeured in grandeur
at his insistence.
Whilst staying with friends
bizarre incidents occurred
manoeuvres to marry,
utterly absurd.
Cupid however had other intentions,
yielding to passion, not interventions.
Clad in black, thin and gaunt,
an affectionate kiss, destined to haunt.
Marauders appeared on black shiny steeds,
riding like fury to serve his needs,
no preventing his actions,
aflame with desire,
affections reciprocated,
a roaring fire.

B J Harrison

CATHERINE OF ARAGON

I'm sending a poem of Catherine, who is she you may well say?
Once a young Princess coming from Spain, that far distant land,
When only 15 to marry Prince Arthur, Henry's elder brother,
A fair and gracious princess, with golden hair with reddish tints, and
serene, kind face, Londoners took her to their hearts the princess
from a golden land.
To marry Prince Arthur for political purposes, to unite Spain and
England was King Henry's intent, to gain more golden crowns.
Alas poor Arthur died shortly after they were wed, a young
widow now,
Then brother Henry took her hand and promised love anew,
'Yes my Lord,' she said, with a shy smile, 'I'll wed you too.'
For 20 long yeas, being faithful and true, bearing Henry's children,
Year after year, sadly all dying but one, Henry VIII played Catherine
False, growing tired of all her pious wisdom, first a romp with Bessie
Blount, then Mary Boleyn, then last but not least the one Anne Boleyn,
Catherine suffered one grievous blow after another,
losing Henry to Anne.
Moving to damper and damper conditions was Henry's orders now.
Anne Boleyn gliding by in once Katherine's barge was caught by the
People aghast, 'We'll have no king's whore here!' the people cried,
Catherine still loved by the populace, an uprising was suggested.
'No!' said Catherine, 'we must avert war,' dying so sadly with loyal
Retainers few, Catherine was finally buried in Peterborough Cathedral.
So please spare a prayer for this good queen, Catholic and Protestant,
Alike, remember Catherine.

Hilda Grace Hutchin

THE ILLUSTRIOUS ENCHANTER
(For Richard)

Barriers fall tree-like - washed clean from stormy rain.
Flowering words flutter from her lips as he joins her path.
Ivy twines to their feet, tying them together like a verdigris chain.
And she shudders in the wake of his moonlit eyes that silence the strath.
She inhales deeply his smell of intoxication.
And she shrouds herself in the warmth of the magic he holds in

his being.

She seeks him, calls him, devours him at every occasion.
The sunshine sinks its rays into their barren hearts - rainbow freeing.
She breathes in his beauty, stroking his soul with her life.
Embalming each their minds and hearts with passioned adoration.
Their happiness grips them, tears them, running rife.
Exalted to a heaven of sheer elation.
Peaceful smiles settle on upturned faces, clasping hands to Eden's river,
And delighting in the quickened eclipse of the moon.
Each rejoices in their new joy giver.
Their angels dance to songless tune.
An entity of waiting, painful pyres of flaming hearts, a savage

companion.

Distant voices calling, shackled dreams died stripped and starved.
She hoped for falling stars to find her.
Wished that she could find one, flying down on Gabrielle's wings to

outstretched arms.

The storm calmed, the fires lulled to a sweet hush.
Blazing from fiery chambers she saw him, and she knew.
Her path became clear and lush.
The sky black no more, but pale purple and blue.
Barriers fall tree-like - washed clean from stormy rain.
Flowering words flutter from her lips as he joins her path . . .

She turns to him and smiles, as his mantra.
For The Maiden now at last has found her Illustrious Enchanter.

Rachael Poyle

MY DAD

What can I tell you about my dad?
How can you understand?
This tall and gentle man,
Smiling all the time
This quiet dad of mine,
I remember happy times,
To know I was loved and cared for
We argued most of the time,
But like a rock he always remained
And listened to my problems
And never would complain,
I never will forget you,
Your smiling face,
Your dimples and twinkling eyes,
I'm only sorry I never got to say,
Goodbye
To Dad with love always.

Christie Forfar

LOVE IN YOUR HEART

When love is in your heart
Nothing else exists,
Not even the world.
Your mind is full of life and music
But your head is numb.
Your mind sings songs that no one else hears.
Silver lights twinkle in your eyes
A lovely tone comes from your lips
And a beautiful sound is always heard.
What is this world called love?
Is it make believe only in the heavens
Or is it for real that comes with life?
Who knows?

L Wright

WEDDING SONG

Love sometimes does pass our little lives
and stops and speaks: Get up and follow me.
We look up, into each other's eyes,
get up, leave all and follow hand in hand.
There is a love that's larger than the sun,
it knows the shade, the night, it knows no end,
it's definite and infinite, it flows
through our hearts, till two are truly one.

Christina Egan

POEM FOR THE QUEEN MOTHER

The striking light blue we remember her by
The famous hat she was proud to wear
These were her days of history and glory
The final last goodbye, her majesty has died.
Warm and peaceful in her sleep, heaven has called
The coffin lay honouring her time and patience
She gave people, who throw flowers and
Remembered her kindness, the prince loved her dearly,
The children remember their granny
They loved her and her sense of fun dearly
The funeral pipes and drums,
What a day to remember, the skies and sun shone,
What a day to remember, heaven has come.

Jean Davy

FOR THE LOVE THAT IS MEANT TO BE

I'll love you more upon the break of this
particular day?
Our destiny's are entwined
criss crossing life's well trodden path?
Beside the crystal clear waters
that match the sparkle in your eyes
do I guess, do I choose?
Are you ready for what is about to come?
The whirl wind of change with the autumn tints
that are yet to come?
Come band with me upon a union of gold
may the frost in your heart slowly thaw
maybe not this year, maybe next hey?
Just let go of all that hate cast your fate upon
the calling beckoning that's so prevalent in the winds
of change
I feel it even more believe you me
this feeling is no longer strange to me!
Please, please open up to me
Will you marry me?

Jonathan Covington

CROSSING OVER

When the Old Man died
I kept the epilogue:
Condolences from relatives,
Acquaintances,
Necessary formal eulogies
Of out-reach family tendrils curling back;
Instinctive pause for final shoulder-glance
From timeshare partners on adjacent tracks.
Inky obituaries - all laudatory -
Colleagues from his academic age,
Day-chant friends rehearsing evensong,
A hazy flower whose blood I might have shared.
All names, and varying temperatures of tears.

Now by autumn sun
I read again consoling words
From those long past the turnstile change,
And pause in my slow shuffle down
The long, inevitable queue,
Coin ready in my hand,
The fare to pay the river ferryman.

John H Hope

In Heaven's Realm

I wonder where you went, now that you are no longer here.
I hope you went to Heaven . . . Yes, I really do. How would the
King of Heaven speak to you? . . . One who had once been upon the
    throne . . . in life, on the planet Earth.
Does Royalty have a special place? Next to pop stars, politicians
and such like. Could it be that you stand in line along with the rest?
I could imagine you to be quite witty. For an instance,
'I say . . . does one raise one's arm in order to go to the bathroom . . .
Or does the bathroom come to one? Walking far, was a bit of a bind,
for these last few years . . . before I moved here.
You could perhaps, drive around 'The Place' in a Golden Cloud.
After all, whilst you were alive . . . didn't you drive around in a
Silver Cloud. That was then and this is now.

I hope you are enjoying your retirement, wherever you are.

C J Cayzer

YOU WERE THERE

When I was lost,
When I was scared,
You touched my hand,
And I felt you there.
When I cried,
When nobody cared,
You were my friend,
And you were there.

Sophie Furmage

FROM THE HEART II

You have the look
Of love to give
You have the grace
Of a falling leaf
You have such dignity
With the honesty of youth
You have no doubters
Just your own doubts
You have unfailing eyes
To observe your world
You have captured my heart
Where disorder now reigns.

Warren Brown

STOLEN PRAYER
(Dedicated to Sue Nicholson)

These words that are spoken
are stolen from a prayer,
my heart has been broken
now that you have left my side.

The sky has gone dark
because you were my one temptation,
you were my guiding light
now all I feel is damnation.

Your eyes were brighter than the sun
you know that you were the one,
the only one that made my dreams come true
now all that I have are words from a stolen prayer.

Now my heart is breaking
because your love has been taken,
it has been taken away from me
now all that is left are these words from a stolen prayer.

Chris Barber

HIRAETH

We call it 'hiraeth',
A yearning, a longing
For the land we love,
Our homeland,
Wales.

The beauties of this land,
Its mountains, lakes and rivers,
Its forests and its moors,
Speak to our hearts,
We are homesick.

It draws us back
With a king of magic.
We are attached
By a gossamer thread,
Fine, yet strong,
Its end wrapped tightly,
Inextricably,
Around our hearts.

We are part of this country,
It is part of us,
Inseparable,
Beloved.

The love,
The hiraeth,
That draws its sons and daughters
Back to Wales,
To Cymru,
The land of our fathers.

Roma Davies

FOR IAN

You accept me as I am
The eccentricities: the passion.
You allow me to be.
Content with what is
Might or maybe,
My spirit unfettered: free.

Happy on a rain soaked day
Together on the windswept shore
Warmed by the under tow of love.
By definition united: one.
Wholly committed to each other.
No room for doubt or misgivings.
All fears dispelled.
Tenderness shared. Vows exchanged.

You accept me as I am
As I accept you.

Sarah Allison

BEWITCHED IN LOVE

As the rainbow serpent breathed a breath of life
All of the lakes on planet Earth became shimmering rainbows too.
Then, as the sun rose, in skies of azure blue
The skies were filled with morning stars
Before all of Earth's people celebrated their reunions with life
In every shade and hue.
'Bewitched in love.'

However, many of the gods were displeased
As a goddess of Venus had shot the sun!
The sky darkened, and the air turned cold
Leaving everyone terribly cheeseed
The day the birds stopped singing, along with all of the fun!
'Bewitched in love.'

Finally a goddess of the air, being both fine and fair
Calmed the gods, and a gentle breeze blew again
So, the moons shadow disappeared -
Along with the pouring rain,
'Bewitched in love.'

The lakes and the oceans changed again
From black to a golden shimmering haze
Whilst the sun still shone, beaming down its glorious rays!
The Earth was restored to its natural beauty,
Though not at all in vain,
For all to remain
'Bewitched in love.'

Colette Breeze

REFULGENCE

The beauty of the earth
is in you
in your form
and in your mind
in your shape
and your intentions
your expressive eyes
so kind

The beauty of the earth
surrounds me
when you
are in my view
bringing calm
beyond all measure
your impressive eyes
fired hue

The beauty of the earth
portrays to me
in tints
of textured dew
your voice I
wait to hear again
sough singing leaves
anew

Séamas M Ó Dálaigh

SUBMISSIONS INVITED
SOMETHING FOR EVERYONE

POETRY NOW 2003 - Any subject,
any style, any time.

WOMENSWORDS 2003 - Strictly women,
have your say the female way!

STRONGWORDS 2003 - Warning!
Age restriction, must be between 16-24,
opinionated and have strong views.
(Not for the faint-hearted)

All poems no longer than 30 lines.
Always welcome! No fee!
Cash Prizes to be won!

Mark your envelope (eg *Poetry Now) 2003*
Send to:
Forward Press Ltd
Remus House, Coltsfoot Drive,
Peterborough, PE2 9JX

OVER £10,000 POETRY PRIZES
TO BE WON!

Judging will take place in October 2003